SIMPLE, EASY CANDY RECIPES

PUBLICATIONS INTERNATIONAL, LTD.

ISBN: 1-56173-281-8

Pictured on front cover: Simple, Molded Candy (*page 26*), Almond-Coconut Balls (*page 90*), Mint Truffles (*page 50*), Layered Fudge (*page 14*), Apricot Balls (*page 84*), Chocolate-Dipped Strawberries (*page 44*), Lollipops (*page 35*), German Chocolate No-Cook Fudge (*page 14*) and Pecan Rolls (*page 28*).

Pictured on back cover, clockwise from top left: Apricot Balls and Chocolate-Covered Raisins (*page 84*); Peanut Butter Confections and Chocolate-Granola Bars (*page 66*) and Toasted Almond Bark (*page 71*); White Chocolate-Dipped Apricots and Stuffed Pecans (*page 38*); Chocolate Peppermints and Chocolate-Nut Squares (*page 42*).

Printed and bound in U.S.A.

8   7   6   5   4   3   2   1

Microwave cooking times in this book are approximate. These recipes have been tested in 650- to 700-watt microwave ovens. Candies cooked in lower-wattage ovens may require longer cooking times. Use the cooking times as guidelines and check for doneness before adding more time.

SIMPLE, EASY CANDY RECIPES

Candy Basics

All of us have a sweet tooth—and what better way to satisfy it than with your own homemade candy, especially when it's so easy to make and so delicious to eat. This book is filled with all kinds of candies—fudges, brittles, bars and truffles—in flavors from chocolate to fruit to butterscotch.

The candies in this book are both cooked and uncooked. Cooked candies are made with a boiling syrup made from sugar (white or brown), a liquid and a variety of ingredients for flavoring, such as chocolate, butter, nuts, dried fruits and extracts. The proportions of the ingredients and the final cooking temperature give cooked candies their seemingly infinite variety of texture, shape and flavor.

Uncooked candies can include a wide variety of ingredients, such as melted chocolate, dried fruits, nuts, marshmallows, condensed or evaporated milk and extracts. These candies are very easy and quick to make—just mix, set and enjoy.

COOKED CANDIES

Most of the classic candies—fudges, fondants, penuches, divinities and brittles—are cooked candies. They are prepared the conventional way on the range-top in a heavy-gauge saucepan and are cooked to the proper temperature. (The higher the temperature the firmer and more brittle the candy will be.) Many candies can also be prepared in the microwave oven.

There are three important things to remember when preparing cooked candies. First, it is necessary to prevent large sugar crystals from forming since they cause the candy to become grainy. To prevent large crystals, the sugar should be completely dissolved and

the crystals should be washed down from the side of the pan before candy thermometer is placed in the pan.

To wash down the crystals from the side of a pan, use a pastry brush dipped into hot water. Gently brush the crystals down into the syrup or collect them on the brush bristles. Dip the brush frequently into hot water to clean off the bristles. (If you do not have a pastry brush, wrap a strip of paper towel around a fork, dip in hot water and wash down the side. Redip in water as needed.) Another easy way to wash down the crystals is to place a lid on the pan for 2 to 3 minutes. This allows the trapped steam to wash down any crystals. If you use the pan lid, make sure the syrup does not boil over.

Second, it is important to cook candy to the correct temperature. If you make cooked candy often, a candy thermometer is a must. They are available in the housewares section of large department stores. Test the accuracy of your candy thermometer before using. (See Equipment section on page 7 for candy thermometer test.) If a candy thermometer is not available, use the cold water test. (See photographs on page 5.) The shape, size and thickness of the pan as well as the cooking temperature will determine the time required for the syrup to reach the final temperature.

Third, candies, such as fudges, must be cooled to lukewarm before beating and shaping. This cooling can take almost two hours for large fudge recipes and patience is necessary. The hot candy can be poured into a heat-proof bowl, such as a stainless steel bowl for a heavy-duty electric mixer, and placed in another bowl of cold water to speed cooling. Caution: Do not get water in the candy. *Do not place the hot candy in the refrigerator or freezer to cool.*

Beat the cooled candy with a heavy-duty electric mixer or wooden spoon until it is no longer shiny or glossy and starts to firm up. This may take from 10 to 30 minutes, depending on the type and volume of candy. At this point, immediately pour the candy into a pan and score into squares or drop onto waxed paper. If it sets up before being spooned out, most fudges, divinity and pralines can be softened by adding about 1 tablespoon hot water and beating again for just a few moments.

Cold Water Test for Candy

Place a small amount of the hot syrup into a cup of cold (but not iced) water. Using your fingers, remove the cooled syrup. If the syrup has not reached the desired ball or thread-stage, continue cooking the candy and test again.

Soft-ball stage (234° to 240°F): The syrup can be rolled into a soft ball that flattens when removed from water.

Firm-ball stage (244° to 248°F): The syrup can be rolled into a firm ball that does not flatten immediately when removed from water.

Hard-ball stage (250° to 266°F): The syrup can be rolled into a firm ball that gives some resistance when pressed.

Soft-crack stage (270° to 290°F): The syrup can be stretched into threads that are hard but elastic.

Hard-crack stage (300° to 310°F): The syrup forms threads that are thin, hard and brittle and can easily be snapped in half.

UNCOOKED CANDIES

Uncooked candies can be as rich and creamy as cooked candies or a combination of chewy, chunky or interesting ingredients. Fudge, truffles, nut clusters, peanut butter cups, bourbon balls and stuffed or chocolate-dipped fruits are examples of uncooked candies. The ingredients for uncooked candies are mixed together, then shaped into balls, pressed into pans, coated or molded in special candy molds. Ingredients typically used for uncooked candies are: fruits, nuts, sweetened condensed milk, evaporated milk, powdered sugar, melted chocolate or confectioner's coating. Some uncooked candies are mixed with, topped with or coated with melted chocolate. While a heat source is needed to melt the chocolate, these candies are still considered uncooked.

CANDY INGREDIENTS

Sugars

Granulated, brown and powdered sugars are used in making candy. Brown sugar, either light or dark, adds its own distinctive flavor. Brown sugar contains a small amount of acid, which may cause candies containing milk to curdle while cooking. This will not affect the final product. Powdered sugar is often used in uncooked candies as it gives the candy a smooth texture.

Corn syrup, molasses and honey are liquid forms of sugar used in candy making. In cooked candies, corn syrup is added to prevent graininess (sugar crystal formation), but too much can make the candy too soft or sticky. Molasses and honey both add a distinctive flavor as well as sweetness.

Dairy Products

Milk is used in many candies. Whole milk gives candy a richer flavor than low-fat milk.

Whipping or heavy cream is used in many candies to add flavor and also add richness. Half-and-half and light cream are also used.

Sweetened condensed milk is whole milk that has about 50 percent of the water removed and sugar added during processing. There is no substitute. It adds flavor and sweetness to both cooked and uncooked candies.

Evaporated milk is whole milk that has about 60 percent of the water removed during processing. It is used undiluted.

Nonfat dry milk is milk that has had the fat and water removed to yield a powder. The powder keeps for long periods without refrigeration. It is often used in uncooked candies to add flavor and texture.

Butter is preferred in most candy recipes because of its flavor. However margarine can be substituted, if desired.

Chocolate

Unsweetened, baking or bitter chocolate is pure chocolate with no sugar or flavorings added. It is commonly available in individually wrapped 1-ounce squares.

Semisweet chocolate is pure chocolate combined with sugar and extra cocoa butter. It is sold in 1-ounce squares, bars, chips and chunks.

Milk chocolate is pure chocolate with sugar, extra cocoa butter and milk solids added. It is available in various shapes—bars, chips, stars, etc.

White chocolate is not considered real chocolate since most or all of the cocoa butter has been removed and replaced by another vegetable fat. White chocolate is available in bars, blocks, disks, chips and chunks.

Unsweetened cocoa powder is formed by extracting most of the cocoa butter from pure chocolate and grinding the remaining chocolate solids into a powder. It contains no sugar or flavoring. Do not use instant cocoa mix since it contains cocoa, sugar, flavoring, an emulsifier and sometimes nonfat dry milk. This cannot be substituted for unsweetened cocoa powder.

Melting Chocolate

Make sure the utensils you use for melting are completely dry. Moisture makes the chocolate become stiff and grainy. If this happens, add ½ teaspoon shortening (not butter) for each ounce of chocolate and stir until smooth. Chocolate scorches easily, and once scorched it cannot be used. Follow one of these three methods for successful melting.

Direct Heat: Place the chocolate in a heavy saucepan over very low heat. Stir constantly and remove from the heat as soon as it melts to prevent scorching.

Double Boiler: This method prevents scorching. Simply place the chocolate in the top of a double boiler or in a bowl over hot, not boiling, water; stir until smooth.

Microwave Oven: Place an unwrapped 1-ounce chocolate square or 1 cup of chips in a small microwavable bowl. Microwave on HIGH 1 to 1½ minutes, stirring after 1 minute. Be sure to stir microwaved chocolate since it holds its shape when melted. Times may differ with low-wattage ovens.

Other Ingredients

Confectioner's or compound coating is not a true chocolate, but may have chocolate flavor added. Compound coatings contain vegetable oil, sugar, milk solids, flavoring and color. They are easy to use for dipping candies and for molding.

Nuts, dried fruits and coconut are added to many candies. These should be fresh for the best flavor. Store leftovers in an airtight container in the refrigerator or freezer.

Flavorings, such as extracts and oils, are commonly used in candies. They are available in supermarkets and pharmacies. When purchasing oils from a pharmacy, check with the pharmacist to make sure that the oils are suitable for internal use. Citrus zests, fruit- and coffee-flavored liqueurs, and instant coffee can also be added to candies. Fresh fruit juices are often too weak to use, but concentrated fruit juices are sometimes added for fruit flavor.

Salt adds flavor of its own and enhances other flavors.

EQUIPMENT

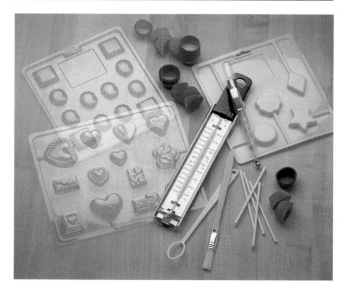

Most kitchens contain all the equipment needed for successful candy making, especially if you only make candy occasionally or make uncooked candy. However, if you make candy often there are some pieces of equipment that will streamline preparations. Check the housewares sections of stores carrying candy making supplies for the items that follow.

Candy thermometers are the most accurate way to tell the temperature of boiling syrup. Always attach the thermometer to the side of the pan after washing down the sugar crystals, making sure the thermometer does not touch bottom of the pan. Read the thermometer at eye level. Before each use, verify your candy thermometer's accuracy by checking its reading in boiling water. Water normally boils at 212°F at sea level. If the thermometer does not read 212°F, you may not live at sea level or the thermometer may be slightly off. (Water always boils at a lower temperature above sea level, because there is less air pressure.)

To adjust the temperature given in a recipe, add or subtract the difference from 212°F as needed. For example, if your thermometer reads 210°F in boiling water and the recipe temperature is 240°F, cook the candy to 238°F or two degrees less than the temperature stated in the recipe.

Saucepans should have a flat bottom and heavy gauge to prevent candy from scorching during cooking. Pan size is important; pans should be large enough to prevent syrups from boiling and foaming over the rim. Syrup increases in volume as it cooks—those containing milk increase about three times during cooking. Watch boiling mixtures carefully and pour into a larger pan, if necessary. A tall narrow pan will increase the cooking time because the evaporation of the liquid will take longer.

Dipping forks or spoons are helpful in dipping candy in melted chocolate or confectioner's coating.

Candy molds, in metal and plastic, are available for hard candies and chocolates. Lollipop molds allow the stick to be put in place before pouring in the candy.

Heavy-duty electric mixers (not portable mixers) are recommended for beating fudges and other candy. A sturdy wooden spoon can also be used.

Candy cases or petit four cases are small paper or foil cups. They are available in different colors and designs.

Pot holders are a must when making cooked candy. The syrup is extremely hot.

Recipes should be read thoroughly before you start. Follow directions exactly.

FABULOUS ❋ FUDGES

*Top plate: Marbled Fudge (page 12); Bottom plate and napkin:
Cocoa Fudge (page 13); Marble: Layered Fudge (page 14)*

Double Chocolate-Creme Fudge

Semisweet and milk chocolate combine to make this dark chocolate fudge.

> 1 can (12 ounces) evaporated milk
> 2 cups (11½ ounces) milk chocolate chips
> 1 cup (6 ounces) semisweet chocolate chips
> 1 jar (7 ounces) marshmallow creme
> ¼ cup butter or margarine
> 4 cups sugar
> Dash salt
> 1 teaspoon vanilla
> 2½ to 3 cups chopped pecans, divided

1. Butter 13×9-inch pan; set aside. Lightly butter side of heavy, large saucepan.

2. Combine evaporated milk, both chips, marshmallow creme, butter, sugar and salt in prepared saucepan. Cook over medium heat, stirring constantly, until sugar dissolves and mixture comes to a boil. Wash down side of pan with pastry brush frequently dipped in hot water to remove sugar crystals.

3. Add candy thermometer. Stir mixture occasionally. Continue to cook until mixture reaches the soft-ball stage (238°F).

4. Pour into large heat-proof mixer bowl. Cool to lukewarm (about 110°F).

5. Add vanilla and beat with heavy-duty electric mixer until thick. Beat in 1 cup of the chopped pecans when candy starts to lose its gloss. Immediately spread in prepared pan. Sprinkle remaining chopped pecans over fudge; gently press into fudge. Score fudge into squares with knife. Refrigerate until firm.

6. Cut into squares. Store in refrigerator.   *Makes about 4 pounds*

Chocolate Cream Cheese Fudge

Cream cheese and melted chocolate combine in this easy no-cook fudge!

> 1 package (3 ounces) cream cheese, softened
> 2 tablespoons milk
> 1 teaspoon vanilla
> 2 cups powdered sugar
> ½ cup semisweet chocolate chips, melted

1. Butter 9×5-inch loaf pan; set aside.

2. Beat cream cheese in medium bowl with electric mixer until light and fluffy; beat in milk and vanilla. Stir in sugar.

3. Cool melted chips until just barely warm; beat into cream cheese mixture. Press into prepared pan. Score fudge into squares with knife. Refrigerate until firm.

4. Cut into squares. Store in refrigerator.   *Makes about 1 pound*

Sour Cream Fudge

The wonderful flavor of this cooked fudge makes the effort worthwhile.

> ¾ **cup sour cream**
> ¼ **cup milk**
> 2 **tablespoons corn syrup**
> 2 **tablespoons butter or margarine**
> 2 **cups sugar**
> 1 **teaspoon vanilla**
> ½ **cup walnut halves (optional)**

1. Butter 8-inch square pan; set aside. Lightly butter side of heavy, medium saucepan.

2. Combine sour cream, milk, corn syrup, butter and sugar in prepared saucepan. Cook over medium heat, stirring constantly, until sugar dissolves and mixture comes to a boil. Wash down side of pan with pastry brush frequently dipped in hot water to remove sugar crystals.

3. Add candy thermometer. Continue to cook until mixture reaches the soft-ball stage (238°F).

4. Pour into large heat-proof mixer bowl. Cool to lukewarm (about 110°F).

5. Add vanilla and beat with heavy-duty electric mixer until thick. Spread into prepared pan. Score fudge into small squares with knife. Refrigerate until firm.

6. Cut into squares. Place walnut half on each piece. Store in refrigerator.

Makes about 1¼ pounds

Marbled Fudge

Each bite contains the great flavors of both white and dark chocolate.

> 2 **cups (12 ounces) semisweet chocolate chips**
> 1 **can (14 ounces) sweetened condensed milk,**
>   **divided**
> 1 **teaspoon vanilla**
> 6 **ounces white chocolate, coarsely chopped**

1. Butter 8-inch square pan; set aside.

2. Melt chocolate chips in heavy, small saucepan over very low heat, stirring constantly. Stir in 1 cup of the condensed milk and the vanilla.

3. At the same time, melt white chocolate in small bowl over hot, not boiling water, stirring constantly. Stir in remaining condensed milk.

4. Pour semisweet chocolate mixture into prepared pan. Pour white chocolate mixture over top. Swirl white chocolate into semisweet chocolate, using a two-prong long-handled fork. Score fudge into squares with knife. Refrigerate until firm.

5. Cut into squares. Store in refrigerator.

Makes about 2 pounds

Cocoa Fudge

Made with cocoa instead of chocolate, this sensational fudge has a rich chocolaty flavor.

 2 cups sugar
⅓ cup unsweetened cocoa powder
¾ cup evaporated milk
¼ cup butter or margarine
 3 tablespoons corn syrup
 1 teaspoon vanilla
½ cup chopped nuts

1. Butter 8-inch square pan; set aside. Lightly butter side of heavy, medium saucepan.

2. Combine sugar and cocoa in small bowl until well mixed. Combine evaporated milk, butter, corn syrup and sugar mixture in prepared saucepan. Cook over medium heat, stirring constantly, until sugar dissolves and mixture comes to a boil. Wash down side of pan with pastry brush frequently dipped in hot water to remove sugar crystals.

3. Add candy thermometer. Stir mixture occasionally. Continue to cook until mixture reaches the soft-ball stage (238°F).

4. Pour into large heat-proof mixer bowl. Cool to lukewarm (about 110°F).

5. Add vanilla and beat with heavy-duty electric mixer until thick. Beat in nuts when candy starts to lose its gloss. Immediately spread in prepared pan. Score fudge into squares with knife. Refrigerate until firm.

6. Cut into squares. Store in refrigerator.   *Makes about 1¼ pounds*

Carob Fudge

Carob is not a true chocolate, but is often used as a chocolate substitute.

 2 cups (12 ounces) unsweetened carob chips
 1 can (14 ounces) sweetened condensed milk
½ cup chopped pecans
 1 teaspoon vanilla

1. Butter 9-inch square baking pan; set aside.

2. Melt carob chips in heavy, small saucepan over very low heat, stirring constantly. Remove from heat.

3. Stir in condensed milk, pecans and vanilla until combined. Spread in prepared pan. Score fudge into squares with knife. Refrigerate until firm.

4. Cut into squares. Store in refrigerator. Bring to room temperature before serving.   *Makes about 1½ pounds*

Hint: Carob chips can be found in natural food stores.

German Chocolate No-Cook Fudge

This is rich with chocolate flavor—a real favorite with chocoholics.

**3 packages (4 ounces each) German sweet
    chocolate, broken into pieces
1 cup (6 ounces) semisweet chocolate chips
1 can (14 ounces) sweetened condensed milk
1 cup chopped pecans
2 teaspoons vanilla
36 pecan halves (optional)**

1. Butter 8-inch square pan; set aside.

2. Melt chocolate and chips in heavy, small saucepan over very low heat, stirring constantly. Remove from heat.

3. Stir in condensed milk, chopped pecans and vanilla until combined. Spread in prepared pan. Arrange pecan halves on fudge. Score fudge into squares with knife. Refrigerate until firm.

4. Cut into squares. Store in refrigerator. Bring to room temperature before serving. *Makes about 2 pounds*

Layered Fudge

Two layers—one butterscotch and nuts, the other chocolate and marshmallows—make this fudge a favorite.

**1 cup (6 ounces) semisweet chocolate chips
1 can (14 ounces) sweetened condensed milk,
    divided
1 teaspoon vanilla
1 cup miniature marshmallows
2 cups (12 ounces) butterscotch chips
½ cup chopped pecans**

1. Butter 8-inch square pan; set aside.

2. Melt chocolate chips in heavy, small saucepan over very low heat, stirring constantly. Remove from heat. Stir in ¾ cup of the condensed milk and the vanilla until smooth. Stir in marshmallows; pour into prepared pan. Refrigerate until firm.

3. Meanwhile, melt butterscotch chips in heavy, small saucepan over very low heat, stirring constantly. Remove from heat; stir in remaining condensed milk until smooth. Stir in pecans.

4. Cool mixture to room temperature; spoon over chocolate layer. Score fudge into squares with knife. Refrigerate until firm.

5. Cut into squares. Store in refrigerator. *Makes about 2 pounds*

Hint: For a different look, prepare butterscotch layer first, then top with chocolate layer.

German Chocolate No-Cook Fudge

Buttermilk Fudge

The sugar caramelizes during cooking to develop a golden color and rich flavor.

> 1 cup buttermilk
> 1 teaspoon baking soda
> 2 tablespoons corn syrup
> 2 tablespoons butter or margarine
> 2 cups sugar
> 1 teaspoon vanilla
> 1 cup chopped pecans

1. Butter 8-inch square pan. Lightly butter side of 3-quart saucepan.

2. Combine buttermilk and baking soda in prepared saucepan, then add corn syrup, butter and sugar. Cook over medium heat, stirring constantly, until sugar dissolves and mixture comes to a boil. Wash down side of pan with pastry brush frequently dipped in hot water to remove sugar crystals.

3. Add candy thermometer; reduce heat to low. Stir mixture occasionally. Continue to cook until mixture reaches the soft-ball stage (238°F).

4. Pour into large heat-proof mixer bowl. Cool to lukewarm (about 110°F).

5. Add vanilla and beat with heavy-duty electric mixer until thick. Beat in pecans when candy starts to lose its gloss. Spread in prepared pan. Score fudge into squares with knife. Refrigerate until firm. Cut into squares. Store in refrigerator.   *Makes about 1 pound*

Note: Mixture boils up! Make sure to use a large (3-quart) saucepan.

Brown Sugar Fudge

Brown sugar is the secret ingredient in this fudge.

> ¾ cup evaporated milk
> 1 tablespoon corn syrup
> 1 cup packed brown sugar
> ¾ cup granulated sugar
> 1½ cups miniature marshmallows
> 1 cup (6 ounces) semisweet chocolate chips
> ¾ cup chopped walnuts or pecans
> 1 teaspoon vanilla

1. Butter 8-inch square pan. Lightly butter side of heavy, medium saucepan.

2. Combine evaporated milk, corn syrup, brown sugar and granulated sugar in prepared saucepan. Cook over medium heat, stirring constantly, until sugar dissolves and mixture comes to a boil. Wash down side of pan with pastry brush frequently dipped in hot water to remove sugar crystals. Continue to boil 10 minutes.

3. Meanwhile, combine remaining ingredients in heat-proof bowl. Pour sugar mixture over marshmallow mixture. Stir until chips melt. Spoon into prepared pan. Score fudge into squares with knife. Refrigerate until firm. Cut into squares. Store in refrigerator.   *Makes about 1¾ pounds*

Classic Fudge

This classic cooked fudge recipe is worth the effort—because it's delicious.

> 1 cup milk
> 2 tablespoons corn syrup
> 2 cups sugar
> 1 cup (6 ounces) semisweet chocolate chips
> 2 tablespoons butter or margarine
> 1 teaspoon vanilla
> ½ cup chopped pecans

1. Butter 8-inch square pan; set aside. Lightly butter sides of heavy, medium saucepan.

2. Combine milk, corn syrup, sugar and chips in prepared saucepan. Cook over medium heat, stirring constantly, until sugar dissolves and mixture comes to a boil. Wash down side of pan with pastry brush frequently dipped in hot water to remove sugar crystals.

3. Add candy thermometer. Stir mixture occasionally. Continue to cook until mixture reaches the soft-ball stage (238°F).

4. Pour into large heat-proof mixer bowl. Add butter. Cool to lukewarm (about 110°F).

5. Add vanilla and beat with heavy-duty electric mixer until thick. Beat in pecans when candy starts to lose its gloss. Spread into prepared pan. Score fudge into squares with knife. Refrigerate until firm. Cut into squares. Store in refrigerator.   *Makes about 1 pound*

Eggnog Fudge

Make this during the holiday season when eggnog is available in the stores.

> ¾ cup eggnog
> 2 tablespoons corn syrup
> 2 tablespoons butter or margarine
> 2 cups sugar
> 1 teaspoon vanilla

1. Butter 8-inch square pan. Lightly butter side of heavy, medium saucepan.

2. Combine eggnog, corn syrup, butter and sugar in prepared saucepan. Cook over medium heat, stirring constantly, until sugar dissolves and mixture comes to a boil. Wash down side of pan with pastry brush frequently dipped in hot water to remove sugar crystals.

3. Add candy thermometer. Continue to cook until mixture reaches the soft-ball stage (238°F).

4. Pour into large heat-proof mixer bowl. Cool to lukewarm (about 110°F).

5. Add vanilla and beat with heavy-duty electric mixer until thick. Spread into prepared pan. Score fudge into squares with knife. Refrigerate until firm. Cut into squares. Store in refrigerator.   *Makes about 1 pound*

Coconut Fudge

This unusual fudge is extra easy because it requires no cooking.

**2 packages (3 ounces each) cream cheese,
 softened**
4½ to 5¼ cups powdered sugar
1 cup chopped blanched almonds
1 cup flaked coconut
½ teaspoon coconut extract
Sliced almonds (optional)

1. Butter 8-inch square pan; set aside.

2. Beat cream cheese and enough powdered sugar in a medium bowl with electric mixer to make a stiff, but not dry mixture.

3. Stir in chopped almonds, coconut and coconut extract. Press mixture into prepared pan. Arrange sliced almonds on top; gently press into fudge. Score fudge into squares with knife. Refrigerate until firm.

4. Cut into squares. Store in refrigerator.   *Makes about 2 pounds*

Peanut Butter Fudge

The peanut butter flavor and creamy texture make you think this is a cooked fudge, but it's another easy no-cook candy.

1 cup creamy peanut butter
1 cup sweetened condensed milk
1 cup powdered sugar
1 teaspoon vanilla
½ cup raisins, chopped

1. Butter 8-inch square pan; set aside.

2. Combine peanut butter, condensed milk, powdered sugar and vanilla in medium bowl. Beat with electric mixer until smooth. Stir in raisins. Press into prepared pan. Score fudge into squares with knife. Refrigerate until firm.

3. Cut into squares. Store in refrigerator.   *Makes about 1½ pounds*

Top: Coconut Fudge
Bottom: Peanut Butter Fudge

Marshmallow-Chocolate Fudge

This creamy fudge cooks for less than 10 minutes and requires no beating.

¾ **cup evaporated milk**
2 **tablespoons butter or margarine**
2 **cups sugar**
2 **cups miniature marshmallows**
1 **cup (6 ounces) semisweet chocolate chips**
½ **cup chopped pecans**
1 **teaspoon vanilla**

1. Butter 8-inch square pan; set aside. Lightly butter sides of heavy, medium saucepan.

2. Combine evaporated milk, butter and sugar in prepared saucepan. Cook over medium heat, stirring constantly, until sugar dissolves and mixture comes to a boil. Wash down side of pan with pastry brush frequently dipped in hot water to remove sugar crystals. Continue to boil 5 minutes.

3. Meanwhile, combine remaining ingredients in heat-proof bowl.

4. Pour sugar mixture over marshmallow mixture. Stir until chocolate melts. Spread in prepared pan. Score fudge into squares with knife. Refrigerate until firm.

5. Cut into squares. Store in refrigerator.   *Makes about 1¾ pounds*

Mocha Fudge

Instant coffee adds the hint of mocha to this light chocolate fudge.

¾ **cup whipping cream**
1 **tablespoon corn syrup**
1¾ **cups sugar**
1 **tablespoon instant coffee granules**
1 **cup (½ of 7-ounce jar) marshmallow creme**
1 **cup milk chocolate chips**
½ **cup chopped nuts**
1 **teaspoon vanilla**

Continued

1. Butter 8-inch square pan; set aside. Lightly butter side of heavy, medium saucepan.

2. Combine cream, corn syrup, sugar and coffee granules in prepared saucepan. Cook over medium heat, stirring constantly, until sugar dissolves and mixture comes to a boil. Wash down side of pan with pastry brush frequently dipped in hot water to remove sugar crystals. Continue to boil 5 minutes.

3. Meanwhile, combine marshmallow creme, chips, nuts and vanilla in heat-proof bowl.

4. Pour sugar mixture over marshmallow mixture. Stir until chips melt. Spoon into prepared pan. Score fudge into squares with knife. Refrigerate until firm.

5. Cut into squares. Store in refrigerator.   *Makes about 1³⁄₄ pounds*

Penuche

Rich and creamy with the taste of brown sugar, this fudge is sure to be a hit.

> **1 cup half-and-half**
> **2 tablespoons butter or margarine**
> **2 cups packed brown sugar**
> **1 cup granulated sugar**
> **2 teaspoons vanilla**
> **1 cup chopped pecans**

1. Butter 8-inch square pan; set aside. Lightly butter side of heavy, medium saucepan.

2. Combine half-and-half, butter, brown sugar and granulated sugar in prepared saucepan. Cook over medium heat, stirring constantly, until sugar dissolves and mixture comes to a boil. Wash down side of pan with pastry brush frequently dipped in hot water to remove sugar crystals.

3. Add candy thermometer. Continue to cook until mixture reaches the soft-ball stage (238°F).

4. Pour into large heat-proof mixer bowl. Cool to lukewarm (about 110°F).

5. Add vanilla and beat with heavy-duty electric mixer until thick. Beat in pecans when candy loses its gloss. Spread into prepared pan. Score fudge into squares with knife. Refrigerate until firm.

6. Cut into squares. Store in refrigerator.   *Makes about 1 pound*

CLASSIC
❁
CANDIES

*Clockwise from left: Pralines (page 34), Lollipops (page 35), Coconut
Bonbons (page 34), Butter Mints (page 30), Coconut Bonbons and
Simple, Molded Candies (page 26)*

Butterscotch-Chocolate Divinity

Each bite contains the flavors of both butterscotch and chocolate.

⅓ cup corn syrup
⅓ cup water
2 cups sugar
2 egg whites
⅛ teaspoon cream of tartar
1 teaspoon vanilla
½ cup milk chocolate chips
½ cup butterscotch chips
½ cup chopped nuts

1. Line 2 or 3 baking sheets with buttered waxed paper; set aside.

2. Combine corn syrup, water and sugar in heavy, medium saucepan. Cook over medium heat, stirring constantly, until sugar dissolves and mixture comes to a boil. Wash down side of pan with pastry brush frequently dipped in hot water to remove sugar crystals.

3. Add candy thermometer. Continue to cook until mixture reaches the hard-ball stage (255°F).

4. Meanwhile, beat egg whites and cream of tartar with heavy-duty electric mixer until stiff but not dry.

5. Slowly pour hot syrup into egg whites, beating constantly. Add vanilla; beat until candy forms soft peaks and starts to lose its gloss. Stir in both chips and nuts. Immediately drop tablespoonfuls of candy in mounds on prepared baking sheets. Store in refrigerator in airtight container between layers of waxed paper or freeze up to 3 months. *Makes about 36 pieces*

Uncooked Fondant

Change the flavorings and colorings to make a variety of candies.

3¼ to 3½ cups powdered sugar, divided
½ cup butter or margarine, softened
¼ cup whipping cream
1 teaspoon vanilla *or* ½ teaspoon peppermint extract
Food coloring (optional)

1. Combine 3 cups of the sugar and the butter; beat with electric mixer until smooth. Beat in whipping cream and vanilla. Using your hands, add additional sugar as needed to make a stiff dough.

2. Knead in food coloring, a few drops at a time, until desired color is obtained. Refrigerate 30 minutes. Shape in balls or patties. Store in refrigerator in airtight container. *Makes about 1 pound*

Variation: Knead ¼ cup of chopped dried apricots, candied cherries, dates, figs or nuts into vanilla-flavored fondant.

Butterscotch-Chocolate Divinity

Simple, Molded Candy

Use white confectioner's coating and add your own color, or start with store-bought colored coating.

12 ounces confectioner's coating
Food coloring (optional)

1. Melt confectioner's coating in bowl over hot, not boiling water, stirring constantly. Add food coloring, a few drops at a time, until desired color is obtained.

2. Spoon into molds. Tap molds on countertop to remove bubbles. Refrigerate until firm. Bring to room temperature before unmolding to avoid cracking molds.   *Makes about 24 candies*

Hint: To make two-tone candies, choose molds with sections to allow for layering. Melt coating as directed. Spoon first layer of coating into molds; tap molds on countertop to remove bubbles. Refrigerate until firm. Spoon second layer into molds. Proceed as directed above.

Pine Nut Brittle

Any nut can be used in this brittle, but pine nuts add a new flavor.

1 cup water
1 cup corn syrup
2 cups sugar
¼ teaspoon cream of tartar
¼ teaspoon salt
2 cups pine nuts, peanuts, pecans or cashews
1 tablespoon butter or margarine, cut into pieces
½ teaspoon baking soda

1. Butter 2 baking sheets; set aside.

2. Combine water, corn syrup, sugar, cream of tartar and salt in heavy, medium saucepan. Cook over medium heat, stirring constantly, until sugar dissolves and mixture comes to a boil. Wash down side of pan with pastry brush frequently dipped in hot water to remove sugar crystals.

3. Add candy thermometer. Continue to cook until mixture reaches the soft-ball stage (238°F).

4. Add pine nuts; continue to cook until mixture reaches 295°F. Remove from heat.

5. Stir in butter and baking soda. Immediately pour hot mixture onto prepared baking sheets; stretch as thin as possible, using 2 forks. Break into pieces when cool. Store in airtight container.   *Makes about 2 pounds*

Simple, Molded Candies

Pecan Rolls

These rolls are best eaten fresh, but they can be frozen for up to three months. If desired, make the fondant and freeze overnight, then finish the rolls the next day.

¼ cup corn syrup
¼ cup water
1¼ cups sugar
1 egg white
⅛ teaspoon cream of tartar
1 teaspoon vanilla
1 package (14 ounces) caramels
3 tablespoons water
2 cups coarsely chopped pecans

1. Line 9×5-inch loaf pan with buttered waxed paper; set aside.

2. Combine corn syrup, water and sugar in heavy, small saucepan. Cook over medium heat, stirring constantly, until sugar dissolves and mixture comes to a boil. Wash down side of pan with pastry brush frequently dipped in hot water to remove sugar crystals.

3. Add candy thermometer. Continue to cook until mixture reaches the hard-ball stage (255°F).

4. Meanwhile, beat egg white and cream of tartar with heavy-duty electric mixer until stiff but not dry.

5. Slowly pour hot syrup into egg white, beating constantly. Add vanilla; beat until candy forms soft peaks and starts to lose its gloss. Spoon fondant into prepared pan. Cut in 3 strips lengthwise, then crosswise in center. Freeze until firm.

6. Line baking sheet with waxed paper; set aside.

7. Melt caramels with water in heavy, small saucepan over low heat, stirring occasionally. Arrange pecans on waxed paper.

8. Working quickly, drop 1 piece of the frozen fondant into melted caramels to coat. Roll in pecans to completely coat. Place on prepared baking sheet to set. Repeat with remaining fondant pieces, reheating caramels if mixture becomes too thick.

9. Cut logs into ½-inch slices. Store in refrigerator in airtight container between layers of waxed paper or freeze up to 3 months.

Makes 6 (5-inch) rolls

Hint: For perfect slices, freeze finished rolls before cutting.

Pecan Rolls

Maple-Nut Seafoam

Similar to divinity, but made with brown sugar, this recipe has a rich maple flavor.

½ cup water
¼ cup corn syrup
1½ cups light brown sugar
1 cup granulated sugar
2 egg whites
⅛ teaspoon cream of tartar
1 teaspoon vanilla
½ teaspoon maple flavoring
½ cup chopped walnuts

1. Line 2 or 3 baking sheets with buttered waxed paper; set aside.

2. Combine water, corn syrup, brown sugar and granulated sugar in heavy, medium saucepan. Cook over medium heat, stirring constantly, until sugar dissolves and mixture comes to a boil. Wash down side of pan with pastry brush frequently dipped in hot water to remove sugar crystals.

3. Add candy thermometer. Continue to cook until mixture reaches the hard-ball stage (255°F).

4. Meanwhile, beat egg whites and cream of tartar with heavy-duty electric mixer until stiff but not dry.

5. Slowly pour hot syrup into egg whites, beating constantly. Add vanilla and maple flavoring; beat until candy forms soft peaks and starts to lose its gloss. Stir in walnuts. Immediately drop tablespoonfuls of candy in mounds on prepared baking sheets.

6. Store in refrigerator in airtight container between layers of waxed paper or freeze up to 3 months.   *Makes about 60 pieces*

Butter Mints

Store the melt-in-the-mouth mints overnight to allow the flavors to blend.

¼ cup butter or margarine
¼ cup evaporated milk
1 tablespoon corn syrup
4 cups powdered sugar, sifted
½ teaspoon peppermint extract
Food coloring

Continued

1. Lightly butter side of heavy, medium saucepan.

2. Combine butter, evaporated milk and corn syrup in prepared saucepan. Heat over medium heat until butter melts and mixture comes to a simmer. Remove from heat.

3. Stir in sugar and extract. Add food coloring, a few drops at a time, until desired color is obtained.

4. Knead dough until smooth on surface covered with powdered sugar. Cover and refrigerate overnight.

5. Line baking sheet with buttered waxed paper; set aside.

6. Shape candy into small balls. Place on prepared baking sheet. Press balls with fork to flatten. Or, shape in long roll, about 1 inch in diameter, then cut into ½-inch pieces. Let stand until set.

7. Store in refrigerator in airtight container between layers of waxed paper.

Makes about 24 mints

Divinity

For best flavor and texture eat this traditional divinity soon after it's made. Do not store with other candies.

½ cup corn syrup
½ cup water
2¼ cups sugar
2 egg whites
⅛ teaspoon cream of tartar
1 teaspoon vanilla
½ cup chopped almonds (optional)

1. Line 2 or 3 baking sheets with buttered waxed paper; set aside.

2. Combine corn syrup, water and sugar in heavy, medium saucepan. Cook over medium heat, stirring constantly, until sugar dissolves and mixture comes to a boil. Wash down side of pan with pastry brush frequently dipped in hot water to remove sugar crystals.

3. Add candy thermometer. Continue to cook until mixture reaches the hard-ball stage (255°F).

4. Meanwhile, beat egg whites and cream of tartar with heavy-duty electric mixer until stiff but not dry.

5. Slowly pour hot syrup in egg whites, beating constantly. Add vanilla; beat until candy forms soft peaks and starts to lose its gloss. Stir in almonds. Immediately drop tablespoonfuls of candy in mounds on prepared baking sheets.

6. Store in refrigerator in airtight container between layers of waxed paper or freeze up to 3 months.

Makes about 40 pieces

Almond Toffee

This buttery, crunchy treat will be a family favorite and disappear in a hurry.

> 1¼ cups chopped almonds, divided
> 3 tablespoons water
> 1 tablespoon corn syrup
> 1 cup butter or margarine
> 1 cup packed brown sugar
> 4 chocolate candy bars (1.55 ounces each),
>   broken into pieces

1. Butter 13×9-inch baking pan. Spread ½ cup of the almonds in prepared pan; set aside.

2. Combine water, corn syrup, butter and sugar in heavy, medium saucepan. Cook over medium heat, stirring constantly, until sugar dissolves and mixture comes to a boil. Wash down side of pan with pastry brush frequently dipped in hot water to remove sugar crystals.

3. Add candy thermometer. Continue to cook until mixture reaches the soft-crack stage (290°F).

4. Add remaining ¾ cup almonds; pour hot mixture over almonds in pan. Place chocolate bars over toffee; let melt. Spread evenly. Refrigerate until firm. Break into pieces. Store in airtight container.   *Makes about 1 pound*

Note: Calibrate your candy thermometer (see page 7) before making this candy. While making, watch the syrup carefully since it can easily overcook at high temperatures.

Easy Cooked Fondant

Fondant can be shaped, colored and flavored in many different ways.

> ½ cup corn syrup
> ½ cup butter or margarine
> 4 cups powdered sugar, sifted, divided
> 1 teaspoon vanilla or other flavoring*
> Food coloring (optional)

1. Butter 8-inch square pan; set aside.

2. Combine corn syrup, butter and 2 cups of the sugar in heavy, medium saucepan over medium heat. Bring to a boil, stirring constantly. Stir in remaining 2 cups sugar and vanilla. Pour mixture into prepared pan; cool.

3. Knead in food coloring, a few drops at a time, until desired color is obtained, or divide fondant and color each portion separately. Shape in balls or patties. Store in refrigerator.   *Makes about 1 pound*

Variation: Add ½ teaspoon anise flavoring to half of the fondant; form into ½-inch-thick log, then cut into ½-inch pieces.

*Use 1 teaspoon fruit-flavored extracts or rum or maple flavorings.

Top: Almond Toffee
Bottom: Penuche (page 21)

Coconut Bonbons

Make the centers one day, then dip them in chocolate the next day.

> 2 cups powdered sugar
> 3 tablespoons evaporated milk
> 2 tablespoons butter or margarine, softened
> 1 cup flaked coconut
> 1 teaspoon vanilla
> 1 cup (6 ounces) semisweet chocolate chips
> 1 tablespoon shortening

1. Line baking sheet with waxed paper; set aside.

2. Combine sugar, evaporated milk, butter, coconut and vanilla in medium bowl.

3. Shape into ½-inch balls, using about ½ tablespoonful of mixture; place on prepared baking sheet. Refrigerate until firm.

4. Melt chips with shortening in heavy, small saucepan over very low heat, stirring constantly.

5. Dip bonbons in melted chocolate. Remove excess chocolate by scraping bottom of bonbon across rim of saucepan; return to prepared baking sheet. Refrigerate until firm; store in refrigerator.   *Makes about 24 bonbons*

Pralines

Pralines are a traditional Louisianian candy. The pralines in this recipe are soft and sugary.

> 1 cup half-and-half
> 2 tablespoons corn syrup
> ¼ cup butter or margarine
> 2 cups brown sugar
> 1 cup granulated sugar
> 1 teaspoon vanilla
> 2 cups whole pecans

1. Line 2 or 3 baking sheets with buttered waxed paper; set aside. Lightly butter side of heavy, medium saucepan.

2. Combine half-and-half, corn syrup, butter, brown sugar and granulated sugar in prepared saucepan. Cook over medium heat, stirring constantly, until sugar dissolves and mixture comes to a boil. Wash down side of pan with pastry brush frequently dipped in hot water to remove sugar crystals.

Continued

3. Add candy thermometer. Continue to cook until mixture reaches the soft-ball stage (238°F).

4. Pour into large heat-proof mixer bowl. Cool to lukewarm (about 110°F).

5. Add vanilla and beat with heavy-duty electric mixer until thick. Beat in pecans when candy loses its gloss. Cool slightly, until mixture is firm enough to mound. Immediately drop teaspoonfuls of candy on prepared baking sheets and spread into patties. Refrigerate until firm.

6. Store in refrigerator.   *Makes about 50 pralines*

Hint: If praline mixture becomes firm before all of the mixture is formed into patties, stir in ½ to 1 tablespoon boiling water. The mixture will then be soft enough to shape.

Lollipops

Let your creativity go—use different shapes, colors and flavors.

> **1 cup water**
> **⅔ cup corn syrup**
> **2 cups sugar**
> **½ teaspoon oil of cinnamon, peppermint, anise or cloves***
> **Food coloring**

1. Oil lollipop mold and place lollipop sticks in position or butter 2 baking sheets; set aside.

2. Combine water, corn syrup and sugar in heavy, medium saucepan. Cook over medium heat, stirring constantly, until sugar dissolves and mixture comes to a boil. Wash down side of pan with pastry brush frequently dipped in hot water to remove sugar crystals.

3. Add candy thermometer. Continue to cook until mixture reaches the hard-crack stage (300°F). Remove from heat.

4. Add oil of cinnamon. Add food coloring, a few drops at a time, until desired color is obtained. Spoon hot mixture into prepared molds, making sure top of sticks are covered with syrup. Or, spread on prepared baking sheets and score into squares while still slightly warm.

5. Unmold lollipops or break squares into pieces when firm.
Makes about 1½ pounds

Hint: The candy sets up quickly and should not be divided in more than two parts for coloring and flavoring. Otherwise, it will set before the molds are filled.

*It is helpful to have the exhaust fan on when using these oils since they are volatile and may cause irritation.

CAPTIVATING
❀
CHOCOLATES

Top plate: Raisin Clusters (page 40); Cherry-Chocolate Logs (page 41); Bottom plate: Chocolate Fudge-Peanut Butter Balls (page 40); Coconut-Almond Bars (page 44); Small plate: Double Mint Cups (page 41)

White Chocolate-Dipped Apricots

The sweetness of white chocolate complements the tart apricots.

3 ounces white chocolate, coarsely chopped
20 dried apricot halves

1. Line baking sheet with waxed paper; set aside. Melt white chocolate in bowl over hot, not boiling water, stirring constantly.

2. Dip half of each apricot piece in chocolate, coating both sides. Place on prepared baking sheet. Refrigerate until firm. Store in refrigerator in container between layers of waxed paper. *Makes 20 apricots*

Stuffed Pecans

An attractive addition to a candy plate, these unusual treats are often the first to be selected.

½ cup semisweet chocolate chips
¼ cup sweetened condensed milk
½ teaspoon vanilla
Powdered sugar (about ½ cup)
80 large pecan halves (about)

1. Melt chips in very small saucepan over very low heat, stirring constantly. Remove from heat.

2. Stir in condensed milk and vanilla until smooth. Stir in enough sugar to make stiff mixture. Refrigerate if needed.

3. Place 1 rounded teaspoonful of the mixture on flat side of pecan half. Top with another pecan half. Repeat. Store in refrigerator. *Makes about 40 candies*

Date-Nut Chews

Dates add sweetness and chewiness to these bite-sized chocolates.

1 cup (6 ounces) semisweet chocolate chips
¾ cup sweetened condensed milk
1 teaspoon vanilla
1 cup coarsely chopped pecans
1 cup chopped dates

1. Line baking sheet with buttered waxed paper; set aside. Melt chips with condensed milk and vanilla in heavy, small saucepan over low heat, stirring occasionally. Remove from heat.

2. Stir in pecans and dates. Drop by teaspoonfuls onto prepared baking sheet. Store in refrigerator. *Makes about 32 chews*

White Chocolate-Dipped Apricots; Stuffed Pecans

Chocolate Fudge-Peanut Butter Balls

Milk chocolate and peanut butter are a great combination for peanut butter lovers—and these candies are so easy to do.

2 cups (11½ ounces) milk chocolate chips
¼ cup half-and-half
⅓ cup creamy peanut butter
⅓ cup chopped peanuts

1. Melt chips with half-and-half in heavy, medium saucepan over low heat, stirring occasionally. Whisk in peanut butter until blended. Refrigerate until mixture is firm enough to shape into balls, but still soft, about 30 minutes, stirring occasionally.

2. Spread peanuts on waxed paper.

3. Shape scant 1 tablespoonful of the mixture into 1-inch balls. Roll balls in peanuts.

4. Store in refrigerator.   *Makes about 32 balls*

Raisin Clusters

The combination of the chocolate and raisins will be a family favorite.

1 cup milk chocolate chips
⅓ cup sweetened condensed milk
1 teaspoon vanilla
2 cups raisins

1. Line baking sheet with buttered waxed paper; set aside.

2. Melt chocolate with condensed milk and vanilla in heavy, small saucepan over low heat, stirring occasionally. Remove from heat.

3. Stir in raisins. Drop by teaspoonfuls onto prepared baking sheet. Refrigerate until firm.

4. Store in refrigerator in container between layers of waxed paper.
Makes 30 clusters

Double Mint Cups

Mint lovers with be delighted with this mint chocolate treat.

**1 package (10 ounces) mint chocolate chips
4 ounces mint-flavored Uncooked Fondant
(page 24)**

1. Oil or spray 1-inch candy molds. Or, use double-thickness paper cups or foil cups in mini-muffin pans.

2. Melt chips in heavy, small saucepan over very low heat, stirring constantly.

3. Spoon about ½ tablespoonful of the chocolate into each cup. With back of spoon, bring chocolate up side of each cup.

4. Place ½-inch-thick piece of fondant in each cup.

5. Spoon about ½ tablespoonful of remaining chocolate over fondant. Refrigerate until firm.

6. Unmold if using molds. Store in refrigerator. *Makes about 36 cups*

Hint: To remove paper cups, cut slit in bottom of paper and peel paper up from bottom. Do not peel paper down from top edge.

Cherry-Chocolate Logs

A fudgy center with cherries is surrounded by crunchy pecans.

**1 cup (6 ounces) semisweet chocolate chips
¼ cup sweetened condensed milk
¼ teaspoon almond extract
½ cup quartered maraschino cherries, drained
1 cup coarsely chopped pecans**

1. Melt chips in heavy, small saucepan over very low heat, stirring constantly. Stir in condensed milk and almond extract. Remove from heat.

2. Stir in cherries. Refrigerate until mixture can be shaped into logs, about 15 minutes.

3. Shape into 2 (1½-inch) logs. Roll logs in pecans. Refrigerate until firm.

4. Cut into ½-inch slices. Store in refrigerator. *Makes about ¾ pound*

Chocolate Peppermints

The peppermint extract and crushed peppermint candy give mint flavor and eye appeal to this festive candy.

1 cup (6 ounces) semisweet chocolate chips
1 cup milk chocolate chips
¼ teaspoon peppermint extract
½ cup crushed peppermint candy

1. Line baking sheet with buttered waxed paper; set aside.

2. Melt both chips in heavy, medium saucepan over low heat, stirring constantly. Stir in peppermint extract.

3. Spread mixture in rectangle about ¼ inch thick on prepared baking sheet. Sprinkle with candy; press into chocolate. Refrigerate until almost firm.

4. Cut into squares. Refrigerate until firm before removing from paper.

Makes about 100 mints

Hint: Squares are easier to cut without breaking if chocolate is not completely firm.

Chocolate-Nut Squares

The chewy caramel center is full of nuts and surrounded by chocolate.

1 cup (6 ounces) semisweet chocolate chips
1 cup milk chocolate chips
1 tablespoon shortening
1 package (14 ounces) caramels
2 tablespoons butter or margarine
3 tablespoons milk
2 cups coarsely chopped pecans

1. Line 8-inch square pan with buttered foil; set aside.

2. Melt both chips with shortening in heavy, small saucepan over very low heat, stirring constantly.

3. Spoon half of the chocolate mixture into prepared pan, spreading evenly over bottom and ¼ inch up sides of pan. Refrigerate until firm.

4. Meanwhile, combine caramels, butter and milk in heavy, medium saucepan. Cook over medium heat, stirring constantly. When mixture is smooth, stir in pecans. Cool to lukewarm.

5. Spread caramel mixture evenly over chocolate in pan. Remelt remaining chocolate mixture over very low heat, stirring constantly; spread over caramel layer. Refrigerate until almost firm.

6. Cut into squares. Store in refrigerator. *Makes about 2 pounds*

Hint: Squares are easier to cut without breaking if chocolate is not completely firm.

Chocolate Peppermints;
Chocolate-Nut Squares

Chocolate-Dipped Strawberries

It's important that the strawberries be completely dry before dipping to prevent the chocolate from discoloring.

2 cups (11½ ounces) milk chocolate chips
1 tablespoon shortening
12 large strawberries with stems, rinsed and dried (about)

1. Line baking sheet with waxed paper; set aside.

2. Melt chips with shortening in top of double boiler over hot, not boiling, water, stirring constantly.

3. Dip about half of each strawberry in chocolate. Remove excess chocolate by scraping bottom of strawberry across rim of pan. Place strawberries on prepared baking sheet. Let stand until set.

4. Store in refrigerator in container between layers of waxed paper.

Makes about 12 strawberries

Variation: Melt 8 ounces white chocolate or pastel confectioner's coating. Redip dipped strawberries; leave a portion of the milk chocolate coating showing.

Hint: Stir chopped dried fruits, raisins or nuts into remaining chocolate; drop by tablespoonfuls onto a baking sheet lined with waxed paper.

Coconut-Almond Bars

Make your own candy bars using this very easy and great-tasting recipe.

2 cups powdered sugar, sifted
1 cup flaked coconut
⅓ cup plus 1 tablespoon sweetened condensed
   milk
1 teaspoon vanilla
½ cup milk chocolate chips
½ cup semisweet chocolate chips
1 tablespoon shortening
1 cup blanched whole almonds (about)

1. Line 8-inch square pan with buttered foil.

2. Combine sugar, coconut, condensed milk and vanilla in medium bowl. Press into prepared pan. Refrigerate until firm.

3. Melt both chips with shortening in heavy, small saucepan over low heat, stirring constantly.

4. Spread evenly over coconut mixture in pan. Press almonds into chocolate in rows 1 inch apart. Score into 2×1-inch bars. Refrigerate until almost firm.

5. Cut into bars. Store in refrigerator.

Makes 32 bars

Chocolate-Dipped Strawberries

Chocolate Bonbons

Bring these chocolates to room temperature before serving for the best flavor.

3¾ cups powdered sugar
¾ cup sweetened condensed milk
¼ cup butter or margarine, softened
1½ cups flaked coconut
1 teaspoon vanilla
¼ teaspoon coconut extract
1 cup milk chocolate chips
2 squares (1 ounce each) unsweetened chocolate, chopped
1 tablespoon shortening

1. Line baking sheet with waxed paper; set aside.

2. Combine sugar, condensed milk, butter, coconut, vanilla and coconut extract in medium bowl.

3. Shape scant 1 tablespoonful of the mixture into 1-inch balls; place on prepared baking sheet. Refrigerate 30 minutes.

4. Melt chips and chopped chocolate with shortening in top of double boiler over hot, not boiling, water, stirring occasionally. Cool slightly.

5. Dip bonbons, using dipping fork or wooden skewer, in chocolate to cover. Remove excess chocolate by scraping bottom of bonbons across rim of pan. Return to prepared baking sheet. Reheat chocolate over hot water if it gets too thick. Refrigerate until set, about 30 minutes.

6. Store in refrigerator.   *Makes about 36 bonbons*

Chocolate Peanut Crunch

This is similar to chocolate-coated peanuts, but even easier to make.

1 cup milk chocolate chips
½ cup semisweet chocolate chips
1 tablespoon shortening
2 tablespoons corn syrup
½ cup unsalted roasted peanuts
2 teaspoons vanilla

1. Butter 8-inch square pan; set aside.

2. Melt both chips with shortening and corn syrup in heavy, small saucepan over low heat, stirring constantly.

3. Stir in peanuts and vanilla. Spread into prepared pan, distributing peanuts evenly. Refrigerate until firm.

4. Break into pieces.   *Makes about ¾ pound*

Fudgy Marshmallow Popcorn

For popcorn and chocolate lovers—the fudgy coating is delicious.

- 3½ **quarts popped popcorn**
- 2 **cups sugar**
- 1 **cup evaporated milk**
- ¼ **cup butter or margarine**
- 1 **cup (½ of 7-ounce jar) marshmallow creme**
- 1 **cup (6 ounces) semisweet chocolate chips**
- 1 **teaspoon vanilla**

1. Pour popcorn into large bowl; set aside.

2. Combine sugar, evaporated milk and butter in heavy, medium saucepan. Cook over medium heat, stirring constantly, until sugar dissolves and mixture comes to a boil. Wash down side of pan with pastry brush frequently dipped in hot water to remove sugar crystals. Continue to boil 5 minutes. Remove from heat.

3. Stir in marshmallow creme, chips and vanilla. Stir until chocolate is melted.

4. Pour over popcorn, stirring until completely coated. Spread popcorn on 2 large baking sheets. Refrigerate until firm.   *Makes about 4 quarts*

Hint: Remove any unpopped kernels before measuring the popped popcorn.

Bourbon Balls

To allow flavors to blend, refrigerate these for at least one day before eating.

- 1 **cup powdered sugar**
- 2 **tablespoons unsweetened cocoa powder**
- 2 **cups finely crushed vanilla wafers (about 44 wafers)**
- 1 **cup finely chopped walnuts**
- ¼ **cup bourbon**
- 3 **tablespoons corn syrup**
  Additional sifted powdered sugar for rolling

1. Sift 1 cup powdered sugar and cocoa into medium bowl. Add crushed vanilla wafers and walnuts. Stir bourbon and corn syrup into crumb mixture. Refrigerate until firm enough to shape into balls, about 30 minutes.

2. Shape scant 1 tablespoonful of the mixture into 1-inch balls.

3. Store in refrigerator in airtight container for 2 to 3 days. Before serving, roll in additional powdered sugar.   *Makes 30 balls*

TERRIFIC

❊

TRUFFLES

Box: White Chocolate Truffles (page 50); Easy Orange Truffles (page 56); Plate: Eggnog Truffles (page 52)

Mint Truffles

These truffles are so rich and so easy—everyone will rave about them.

1 package (10 ounces) mint chocolate chips
⅓ cup whipping cream
¼ cup butter or margarine
1 container (3½ ounces) chocolate sprinkles

1. Melt chips with whipping cream and butter in heavy, medium saucepan over low heat, stirring occasionally. Pour into pie pan. Refrigerate until mixture is fudgy, but soft, about 2 hours.

2. Shape about 1 tablespoonful of the mixture into 1¼-inch ball. To shape, roll mixture in your palms. Place balls on waxed paper.

3. Place sprinkles in shallow bowl.

4. Roll balls in sprinkles; place in petit four or candy cases. (If coating mixture won't stick because truffle has set, roll between your palms until outside is soft.)

5. Truffles can be refrigerated 2 to 3 days or frozen several weeks.

Makes about 24 truffles

Hint: Truffles are coated with cocoa, powdered sugar, nuts, sprinkles or cookie crumbs to add flavor and prevent the truffle from melting in your fingers.

White Chocolate Truffles

Made with white chocolate, these soft truffles have lots of orange flavor.

12 ounces white chocolate, coarsely chopped
⅓ cup whipping cream
2 tablespoons orange liqueur
1 teaspoon grated orange zest
1 to 1¼ cups powdered sugar

1. Melt white chocolate with whipping cream in heavy, medium saucepan over low heat, stirring constantly. Whisk in liqueur and zest until blended. Pour into pie pan. Refrigerate until mixture is fudgy, but soft, about 2 hours.

2. Shape about 1 tablespoonful of the mixture into 1¼-inch ball. To shape, roll mixture in your palms. Place balls on waxed paper.

3. Sift sugar into shallow bowl.

4. Roll balls in sugar; place in petit four or candy cases.

5. Truffles can be refrigerated 2 to 3 days or frozen several weeks.

Makes about 36 truffles

Mint Truffles

Marbled Truffles

Can't decide whether to make white or dark chocolate truffles?
Marbled truffles have both.

6 ounces white chocolate, coarsely chopped
½ cup whipping cream, divided
1 teaspoon vanilla
1 cup (6 ounces) semisweet chocolate chips
1 tablespoon butter or margarine
2 tablespoons orange-flavored liqueur
¾ cup powdered sugar, sifted

1. Melt white chocolate with ¼ cup of the whipping cream and the vanilla in heavy, medium saucepan over low heat, stirring constantly. Pour into 9-inch square pan. Refrigerate.

2. Melt semisweet chocolate chips with butter and remaining ¼ cup whipping cream in heavy, medium saucepan over low heat, stirring constantly. Whisk in liqueur.

3. Pour chocolate mixture over refrigerated white chocolate mixture. Refrigerate until mixture is fudgy, but soft, about 1 hour.

4. Shape about 1 tablespoonful of the mixture into 1¼-inch ball. To shape, roll mixture in your palms. Place balls on waxed paper.

5. Sift powdered sugar into shallow bowl.

6. Roll balls in powdered sugar; place in petit four or candy cases. (If coating mixture won't stick because truffle has set, roll between your palms until outside is soft.)

7. Truffles can be refrigerated 2 to 3 days or frozen several weeks.

Makes about 30 truffles

Eggnog Truffles

Unusual but delicious, these creamy truffles are piped—they are
too soft to shape into balls.

2 cups (11½ ounces) milk chocolate chips
2 tablespoons butter or margarine
½ cup eggnog
36 chocolate cups (about), either purchased or
      homemade (recipe follows)

1. Melt chips with butter and eggnog in heavy, medium saucepan over low heat, stirring occasionally. Pour into pie pan. Refrigerate until mixture is thick, but soft, about 2 hours.

2. Spoon truffle mixture into pastry bag fitted with large star tip. Pipe mixture into chocolate cups.

3. Truffles can be refrigerated 2 to 3 days or frozen several weeks.

Makes about 36 truffles

Chocolate Cups

2 cups (12 ounces) semisweet chocolate chips
1 tablespoon shortening

1. Melt chips with shortening in heavy, small saucepan over very low heat, stirring constantly.

2. Spoon about ½ tablespoonful of the chocolate mixture into each of about 36 small foil candy cups. With back of spoon, bring some of the chocolate up side of each cup. Refrigerate until firm.   *Makes about 36 cups*

Hint: To remove foil cups, cut slit in bottom of cup and peel foil up from bottom. Do not peel down from top edge.

Rum Truffles

Flavored with rum extract, these creamy truffles are sure to please.

2 cups (12 ounces) semisweet chocolate chips
½ cup whipping cream
1½ teaspoons rum extract
1 teaspoon vanilla
½ cup powdered sugar
¼ cup unsweetened cocoa powder

1. Melt chips with whipping cream in heavy, medium saucepan over low heat, stirring occasionally. Whisk in rum extract and vanilla until blended. Pour into pie pan. Refrigerate until mixture is fudgy, but soft, about 75 minutes.

2. Shape about 1 tablespoonful of the mixture into 1¼-inch ball. To shape, roll mixture in your palms. Place balls on waxed paper.

3. Sift powdered sugar and cocoa into shallow bowl.

4. Roll balls in sugar-cocoa mixture; place in petit four or candy cases. (If coating mixture won't stick because truffle has set, roll between your palms until outside is soft.)

5. Truffles can be refrigerated 2 to 3 days or frozen several weeks.
Makes about 30 truffles

Shaping truffles: *To give truffles a professional appearance use a one-tablespoon-size scoop with a release, similar to a miniature ice cream scoop. As the scoop is drawn through the truffle mixture, it forms a rough ball shape. The truffle only needs a little additional shaping in your palms to make a perfect ball before coating. Using the scoop also makes your truffles more uniform in size.*

Raspberry Truffles

Using both raspberry jam and raspberry brandy doubles the flavor.

2 cups (12 ounces) semisweet chocolate chips
¾ cup sweetened condensed milk
¼ cup seedless raspberry jam
2 tablespoons butter or margarine
1 tablespoon framboise (raspberry brandy)
3 ounces white chocolate, coarsely chopped

1. Melt chips with condensed milk, jam and butter in heavy, medium saucepan over low heat, stirring occasionally. Whisk in brandy until blended. Pour into pie pan. Refrigerate until mixture is fudgy, but soft, about 1½ hours. Line baking sheet with waxed paper; set aside.

2. Melt white chocolate in bowl over hot, not boiling water, stirring constantly; set aside.

3. Shape about 1 tablespoonful of the mixture into 1¼-inch ball. To shape, roll mixture in your palms. Place balls on prepared baking sheet.

4. Spoon melted white chocolate over top one third of each truffle. Refrigerate until chocolate is firm.

5. Remove from waxed paper; place in petit four or candy cases.

6. Truffles can be refrigerated 2 to 3 days or frozen several weeks.

Makes about 40 truffles

Cream Truffles

Use a variety of cream liqueurs and make up several batches of these truffles.

2 cups (12 ounces) semisweet chocolate chips
¼ cup whipping cream
¼ cup butter or margarine
3 tablespoons cream liqueur
½ to ¾ cup powdered sugar

1. Melt chips with whipping cream and butter in heavy, medium saucepan over low heat, stirring occasionally. Stir in liqueur. Pour into pie pan. Refrigerate until mixture is fudgy, but soft, about 2 hours.

2. Shape about 1 tablespoonful of the mixture into 1¼-inch ball. To shape, roll mixture in your palms. Place balls on waxed paper.

3. Sift sugar into shallow bowl.

4. Roll balls in sugar; place in petit four or candy cases. (If coating mixture won't stick because truffle has set, roll between palms until outside is soft.)

5. Truffles can be refrigerated 2 to 3 days or frozen several weeks.

Makes about 36 truffles

Raspberry Truffles;
Mocha Truffles (page 56)

Mocha Truffles

These cookie-coated truffles have a double dose of coffee flavor.

2 cups (11½ ounces) milk chocolate chips
½ cup whipping cream
2 teaspoons instant coffee granules
2 tablespoons coffee-flavored liqueur
⅔ cup vanilla wafer crumbs (about 15 wafers)

1. Melt chips with whipping cream and coffee granules in heavy, medium saucepan over low heat, stirring occasionally. Whisk in liqueur until blended. Pour into pie pan. Refrigerate until mixture is fudgy, but soft, about 2 hours.

2. Shape about 1 tablespoonful of the mixture into 1¼-inch ball. To shape, roll mixture in your palms. Place balls on waxed paper.

3. Place crumbs in shallow bowl.

4. Roll balls in crumbs; place in petit four or candy cases. (If coating mixture won't stick because truffle has set, roll between your palms until outside is soft.)

5. Truffles can be refrigerated 2 to 3 days or frozen several weeks.

Makes about 30 truffles

For best flavor of truffles: *To enjoy the full flavor of truffles, allow them to come to room temperature before serving.*

Easy Orange Truffles

Not as soft as other truffles, these are easier to shape as well as delicious with their orange-chocolate taste.

1 cup (6 ounces) semisweet chocolate chips
2 squares (1 ounce each) unsweetened chocolate,
** chopped**
1½ cups powdered sugar
½ cup butter or margarine, softened
1 tablespoon grated orange peel
1 tablespoon orange-flavored liqueur
2 squares (1 ounce each) semisweet chocolate,
** grated**

Continued

1. Melt chips and chopped chocolate in heavy, small saucepan over very low heat, stirring constantly; set aside.

2. Combine sugar, butter, orange peel and liqueur in small bowl. Beat with electric mixer until combined. Beat in cooled chocolate. Pour into pie pan. Refrigerate until mixture is fudgy and can be shaped into balls, about 30 minutes.

3. Shape scant 1 tablespoonful of the mixture into 1-inch ball. To shape, roll mixture in your palms. Place balls on waxed paper.

4. Sprinkle grated chocolate in shallow bowl.

5. Roll balls in grated chocolate; place in petit four or candy cases. (If coating mixture won't stick because truffle has set, roll between your palms until outside is soft.)

6. Truffles can be refrigerated 2 to 3 days or frozen several weeks.

Makes about 34 truffles

Peanut Butter Truffles

A peanut butter lover's delight—peanut butter and chocolate blended into a silky treat.

2 cups (11½ ounces) milk chocolate chips
½ cup whipping cream
2 tablespoons butter or margarine
½ cup creamy peanut butter
¾ cup finely chopped peanuts

1. Melt chips with whipping cream and butter in heavy, medium saucepan over low heat, stirring occasionally. Whisk in peanut butter until blended. Pour into pie pan. Refrigerate until mixture is fudgy, but soft, about 1 hour, stirring occasionally.

2. Shape about 1 tablespoonful of the mixture into 1¼-inch ball. To shape, roll mixture in your palms. Place balls on waxed paper.

3. Place peanuts in shallow bowl.

4. Roll balls in peanuts; place in petit four or candy cases. (If coating mixture won't stick because truffle has set, roll between your palms until outside is soft.)

5. Truffles can be refrigerated 2 to 3 days or frozen several weeks.

Makes about 36 truffles

KIDS'

❁

CREATIONS

Canister: Oven Caramel Popcorn (page 62); Plate: Coated Pretzels (page 68), Peanut Butter-Potato Pinwheels (page 70) and Marshmallow Cups (page 71); Napkin: S'Mores (page 65)

Peanut Butter Cups

These cups are so good—with lots of chocolate and peanut butter flavor.

>   2 cups (12 ounces) semisweet chocolate chips
>   1 cup milk chocolate chips
>   1½ cups powdered sugar
>   1 cup crunchy or smooth peanut butter
>   ½ cup vanilla wafer crumbs (about 11 wafers)
>   6 tablespoons butter or margarine, softened

1. Line 12 (2½-inch) muffin cups with double-thickness paper cups or foil cups; set aside.

2. Melt both chips in heavy, small saucepan over very low heat, stirring constantly.

3. Spoon about 1 tablespoonful of the chocolate into each cup. With back of spoon, bring chocolate up side of each cup. Refrigerate until firm, about 20 minutes.

4. Combine sugar, peanut butter, crumbs and butter in medium bowl.

5. Spoon 2 tablespoons of the peanut butter mixture into each chocolate cup. Spread with small spatula.

6. Spoon about 1 tablespoon remaining chocolate over each peanut butter cup. Refrigerate until firm. *Makes 12 cups*

Hint: To remove paper cups, cut slit in bottom of paper and peel paper up from bottom. Do not peel paper down from top edge.

Butterscotch Rocky Road

Children (and adults) often prefer the taste of butterscotch to chocolate.

>   1½ cups miniature marshmallows
>   1 cup coarsely chopped pecans
>   2 cups (12 ounces) butterscotch chips
>   ½ cup sweetened condensed milk

1. Butter 13×9-inch pan. Spread marshmallows and pecans evenly on bottom of pan.

2. Melt butterscotch chips in heavy, medium saucepan over low heat, stirring constantly. Stir in condensed milk.

3. Pour butterscotch mixture over marshmallows and pecans, covering entire mixture. If necessary, use a knife or small spatula to help cover the marshmallows and nuts with butterscotch mixture. Let stand in pan until set.

4. Cut into squares. Store in refrigerator. *Makes about 1 pound*

Left: Peanut Butter Cups
Right: Butterscotch Rocky Road

Caramel-Marshmallow Apples

The marshmallows add additional flavor to this classic treat.

1 package (14 ounces) caramels
1 cup miniature marshmallows
1 tablespoon water
5 or 6 small apples

1. Line baking sheet with buttered waxed paper; set aside.

2. Combine caramels, marshmallows and water in medium saucepan. Cook over medium heat, stirring constantly, until caramels melt. Cool slightly while preparing apples.

3. Rinse and thoroughly dry apples. Insert flat sticks in stem ends of apples.

4. Dip each apple in caramel mixture, coating apples. Remove excess caramel mixture by scraping apple bottoms across rim of saucepan. Place on prepared baking sheet. Refrigerate until firm.   *Makes 5 or 6 apples*

Caramel-Nut Apples: Roll coated apples in chopped nuts before refrigerating.

Caramel-Chocolate Apples: Drizzle melted milk chocolate over coated apples before refrigerating.

Oven Caramel Popcorn

You'll have no storage problem with this one; it disappears as soon as it's made.

4 quarts popped popcorn
½ teaspoon salt
½ cup corn syrup
½ cup butter or margarine
1½ cups packed light brown sugar
1 teaspoon vanilla

1. Preheat oven to 250°F. Combine popcorn and salt in large heat-proof bowl; set aside.

2. Combine corn syrup, butter and sugar in heavy, medium saucepan. Cook over medium heat, stirring constantly, until sugar dissolves. Bring mixture to a boil. Continue boiling 5 minutes over medium heat, stirring often. Remove from heat.

3. Stir in vanilla. Immediately pour sugar mixture over popcorn, stirring until completely coated. Spread popcorn on 1 large baking pan.

4. Bake 1 hour, stirring every 15 minutes. Cool.   *Makes about 4 quarts*

Hint: Remove any unpopped kernels before measuring the popped popcorn.

Clockwise from top right: Caramel-Nut Apple, Caramel-Chocolate Apple and Caramel-Marshmallow Apple

Peanut Butter Treats

Raisins and peanut butter are a terrific flavor combination.

5 cups crisp rice cereal
1 cup raisins
1 cup corn syrup
1 cup sugar
1½ cups creamy peanut butter
1 teaspoon vanilla

1. Butter 13×9-inch baking pan; set aside. Combine cereal and raisins in large heat-proof bowl; set aside.

2. Combine corn syrup and sugar in heavy, medium saucepan. Cook over medium heat, stirring constantly, until sugar dissolves. Remove from heat.

3. Add peanut butter and vanilla, stirring until combined. Pour over cereal-raisin mixture, stirring until combined. Press into prepared pan. Refrigerate until firm.

4. Cut into 2×1-inch bars.

Makes 48 bars

Chocolate Cereal Bars

These bars are great for lunch boxes, after-school snacks or classroom treats.

6 cups crisp rice cereal
1 cup (6 ounces) semisweet chocolate chips
1 jar (7 ounces) marshmallow creme
2 tablespoons butter or margarine
1 teaspoon vanilla

1. Butter 13×9-inch baking pan; set aside. Place cereal in large heat-proof bowl; set aside.

2. Melt chips with marshmallow creme and butter in heavy, small saucepan over medium heat, stirring occasionally. Remove from heat.

3. Stir in vanilla. Pour chocolate mixture over cereal. Stir until blended. Press into prepared pan; cool.

4. Cut into squares.

Makes 24 squares

Honey-Nut Crunch

This quick-and-easy coated popcorn is similar to caramel popcorn.

3 quarts popped popcorn
2 cups pecan halves
½ cup butter
½ cup honey
1 teaspoon vanilla

1. Preheat oven to 350°F. Combine popcorn and nuts in large heat-proof bowl; set aside.

2. Combine butter, honey and vanilla in small saucepan. Cook over medium heat until butter melts.

3. Pour honey mixture over popcorn mixture. Stir until combined. Divide mixture and place on 2 baking sheets.

4. Bake 15 minutes, stirring every 5 minutes, until light golden brown.

Makes about 3 quarts

Hint: Remove any unpopped kernels before measuring the popped popcorn.

S'Mores

Don't reserve these for campfires—they're easy to do in the oven.

8 whole graham crackers, halved crosswise
4 milk chocolate bars (1.55 ounces each), halved
1 cup miniature marshmallows

1. Preheat broiler.

2. Arrange half of the graham crackers on baking sheet. Top each cracker with 1 piece of the chocolate bars. Broil until chocolate is softened, but not melted.

3. Arrange 2 tablespoons of the marshmallows on each cracker. Broil until lightly toasted.

4. Top with remaining crackers and serve.

Makes 8 S'mores

Peanut Butter Confections

Perfect for an after-school snack, these have milk and peanut butter.

1½ cups instant nonfat dry milk
1 cup creamy peanut butter
1 cup honey
1 cup flaked coconut
1 cup graham cracker crumbs *or* 1 cup flaked
   coconut

1. Line baking sheet with waxed paper; set aside.

2. Combine milk, peanut butter, honey and 1 cup coconut in medium bowl. Refrigerate until firm enough to shape into balls, about 30 minutes.

3. Shape scant 1 tablespoonful of the mixture into 1-inch balls.

4. Place crumbs in shallow bowl.

5. Roll balls in crumbs. Place balls on prepared baking sheet. Refrigerate until set.

6. Store in refrigerator in airtight container.   *Makes about 48 balls*

Chocolate-Granola Bars

The granola and fruits are coated with the sweetness of white chocolate.

3 cups raisin-and-nut granola
½ cup finely chopped dried apricots
½ cup finely chopped dates
12 ounces white chocolate, coarsely chopped
¼ cup half-and-half or evaporated milk

1. Butter 8-inch square pan. Combine granola, apricots and dates in medium heat-proof bowl; set aside.

2. Melt white chocolate with half-and-half in heavy, small pan over low heat, stirring constantly.

3. Pour chocolate mixture over granola mixture and stir until coated. Press into prepared pan. Refrigerate until firm.

4. Cut into 2 × 1-inch bars. Store in refrigerator.   *Makes 32 bars*

Top plate: Peanut Butter Confections
Bottom plate: Chocolate-Granola Bars;
Toasted Almond Bark (page 71)

Pastel Popcorn

This can be shaped in balls while still warm or spread into clusters.

2½ **quarts popped popcorn**
½ **cup corn syrup**
⅓ **cup water**
1 **cup sugar**
½ **teaspoon salt**
¼ **cup butter or margarine, cut into pieces**
1 **teaspoon vanilla**
Food coloring

1. Pour popcorn into large heat-proof bowl; set aside.

2. Combine corn syrup, water, sugar and salt in medium saucepan. Cook over medium heat, stirring constantly, until sugar dissolves and mixture comes to a boil. Wash down side of pan with pastry brush frequently dipped in hot water to remove sugar crystals.

3. Add candy thermometer. Continue to cook until mixture reaches the hard-ball stage (255°F). Remove from heat.

4. Whisk in butter and vanilla. Add food coloring, a few drops at a time, until desired color is obtained. Immediately pour sugar mixture over popcorn, stirring until completely coated. Spread popcorn on 2 large baking sheets.

5. Cool slightly and shape in balls or leave as clusters.

Makes about 3 quarts

Hint: Remove any unpopped kernels before measuring the popped popcorn.

Coated Pretzels

The sweetness of the coating and the saltiness of the pretzels make a great combination.

8 **ounces confectioner's coating**
1 **teaspoon shortening**
24 **pretzels (about 3 ounces)**

1. Line baking sheet with waxed paper.

2. Melt coating with shortening in bowl over hot, not boiling water, stirring constantly.

3. Drop pretzels in coating, one at a time. Remove pretzels with fork, allowing excess coating to drip back into bowl. Place on prepared baking sheet. Let stand until firm.

4. Store between layers of waxed paper.

Makes 24 pretzels

Hint: Add raisins to leftover coating. Drop by teaspoonfuls onto baking sheet lined with waxed paper. Let stand until set, about 30 minutes.

Pastel Popcorn

Peanut Butter-Potato Pinwheels

The potato mixture and the peanut butter make a delicious candy.

1 small potato* (3 to 4 ounces), cooked, drained,
mashed and cooled
2 to 3 cups powdered sugar
1 teaspoon vanilla
²/₃ cup creamy peanut butter, room temperature

1. Combine mashed potato, 2 cups powdered sugar and vanilla in medium bowl.

2. Mix in enough of the remaining powdered sugar, a little at a time, until dough can be rolled out.

3. Roll out dough into ¼-inch-thick rectangle on surface covered with powdered sugar.

4. Spread with peanut butter.

5. Roll up, jelly-roll style, starting at one long side. Wrap in plastic wrap; place on a baking sheet and refrigerate until firm, about 2 hours.

6. Cut crosswise into ½-inch slices. Store in refrigerator.

Makes about 1¼ pounds

*If potato is larger or too warm, additional powdered sugar may be needed to make a stiff dough.

Butterscotch Oatmeal Rounds

The flavor of this easy-to-make candy is best after it ages for two days.

½ cup milk
½ cup butter or margarine
1 cup sugar
1½ cups butterscotch chips
3 cups uncooked rolled oats
1 teaspoon vanilla

1. Line baking sheet with waxed paper. Lightly butter side of heavy, medium saucepan.

2. Combine milk, butter, sugar and chips in prepared saucepan. Cook over medium heat, stirring constantly, until mixture comes to a boil. Boil 1 minute. Remove from heat.

3. Stir in oats and vanilla. Cool slightly until mixture mounds. Drop by tablespoonfuls onto prepared baking sheet. Refrigerate 2 days to allow flavors to blend.

4. Store in refrigerator.

Makes about 30 rounds

Toasted Almond Bark

You'll be glad this is so easy to do, because you'll be making another batch soon!

½ cup slivered almonds
12 ounces white chocolate, coarsely chopped
1 tablespoon shortening

1. Preheat oven to 325°F.

2. Spread almonds on baking sheet. Bake 12 minutes or until golden brown, stirring occasionally.

3. Meanwhile, butter another baking sheet. Spread warm almonds on buttered baking sheet.

4. Melt white chocolate with shortening in heavy, small saucepan over very low heat, stirring constantly.

5. Spoon evenly over almonds, spreading about ¼ inch thick. Refrigerate until almost firm.

6. Cut into squares, but do not remove from baking sheet. Refrigerate until firm.   *Makes about 1 pound*

Marshmallow Cups

Kids love these small marshmallow-filled chocolate cups—they're easy to eat.

2 cups (11½ ounces) milk chocolate chips
2 tablespoons shortening
1 cup (½ of 7-ounce jar) marshmallow creme

1. Line 18 mini-muffin cups with double-thickness paper cups or foil cups; set aside.

2. Melt chips with shortening in heavy, small saucepan over very low heat, stirring constantly.

3. Spoon about ½ tablespoonful of the chocolate mixture into each cup. With back of spoon, bring chocolate up side of each cup.

4. Spoon 1 tablespoonful of the marshmallow creme into each chocolate cup, using spoons dipped in hot water. Spread with small spatula.

5. Spoon about ½ tablespoonful of remaining chocolate over each marshmallow cup. Refrigerate until firm.   *Makes 18 cups*

Hint: To remove paper cups, cut slit in bottom of paper and peel paper up from bottom. Do not peel paper down from top edge.

MICROWAVE ❀ MORSELS

Clockwise from top left: Yogurt-Raisin Bars (page 76),
Easy Microwave Fudge (page 77) and Pecan Brittle (page 77)

Butter Toffee Crunch

A cross between toffee and brittle, this has a wonderful buttery flavor.

> ¾ cup butter or margarine
> 1 tablespoon corn syrup
>   Hot water
> 1 cup sugar
> 1 package (2¼ ounces) sliced almonds (about ¾ cup)

1. Place butter in 2-quart microwave-safe bowl. Microwave on HIGH 1 minute or until melted.

2. Stir in corn syrup, 2 tablespoons hot water and sugar. Microwave on HIGH 4 minutes, stirring after 1 minute. Add 1 tablespoon hot water; stir to combine. Microwave on HIGH 1 minute.

3. Stir in almonds. Microwave on HIGH 2 to 3 minutes, until light caramel in color.

4. Pour onto an ungreased baking sheet. Spread out candy. Cool until set.

5. Break into pieces. Store in airtight container.   *Makes about ¾ pound*

Variation: Sprinkle hot candy with 1 cup milk chocolate chips. Let melt; spread.

Hint: If kitchen is cold, warm baking sheet before pouring out toffee. It will spread more easily and be thinner.

Glazed Almonds

The almonds are lightly coated with a translucent sweetness.

> 1 cup blanched whole almonds (about 5 ounces)
> ⅓ cup water
> 1 tablespoon corn syrup
> 1 cup sugar

1. Spread almonds in microwave-safe pie pan. Microwave on HIGH 3 minutes, stirring after every minute. Almonds should be lightly toasted.

2. Butter baking sheet; set aside. Lightly butter side of microwave-safe 2-quart dish.

3. Combine water, corn syrup and sugar in prepared 2-quart dish. Microwave on HIGH 2 minutes; stir. Microwave on HIGH 5 minutes.

4. Using dipping fork or table fork, dip almond in syrup. Remove excess syrup by scraping bottom of almonds across rim of dish. Place almonds on prepared baking sheet. (If syrup begins to harden, microwave on HIGH 1 minute; stir.) Cool at room temperature until set.

5. Store loosely covered at room temperature.   *Makes about 1 cup*

Top: Butter Toffee Crunch
Bottom: Glazed Almonds

Yogurt-Raisin Bars

Plump, fresh raisins are the best choice for this quick-to-make candy.

2 cups white chocolate, coarsely chopped
¼ cup plain yogurt, room temperature
1 teaspoon vanilla
2½ cups golden or dark raisins

1. Line 8-inch square pan with buttered foil; set aside.

2. Place white chocolate in small microwave-safe bowl. Microwave on MEDIUM 2 minutes, stirring after every minute. Stir until smooth. If not completely melted, microwave on MEDIUM 30 seconds more.

3. Stir in yogurt and vanilla until smooth. Stir in raisins. Press into prepared pan. Refrigerate until set.

4. Remove candy from pan by lifting out foil. Cut into 2×1-inch bars. Store in refrigerator.
Makes 32 bars

Peanut Butter Rocky Road Fudge

This light-colored candy has peanuts, raisins and marshmallows in it.

2 cups (12 ounces) peanut butter chips
⅓ cup sweetened condensed milk
1 tablespoon corn syrup
2 cups miniature marshmallows
¼ cup salted peanuts
¼ cup raisins

1. Line 9-inch square pan with buttered foil; set aside. Lightly butter 2-quart microwave-safe dish.

2. Combine chips, milk and corn syrup in prepared 2-quart dish. Microwave on HIGH 1 minute; stir. If chips are not melted, microwave on HIGH 1 minute more; stir.

3. Immediately stir in marshmallows, peanuts and raisins. Press into prepared square pan. Score fudge with knife. Refrigerate overnight.

4. Remove fudge from pan by lifting out foil. Cut into squares. Store in refrigerator.
Makes about 1½ pounds

Pecan Brittle

The pecans are toasted until crunchy and the finished brittle is light and easy to break.

> ½ cup corn syrup
> 1 cup sugar
> 1 cup pecan halves
> 1 tablespoon butter or margarine, cut into pieces
> 1 teaspoon vanilla
> 1½ teaspoons baking soda

1. Butter large baking sheet; set aside.

2. Combine corn syrup and sugar in 2-quart microwave-safe bowl. Stir in pecans. Microwave on HIGH 5 to 5½ minutes until syrup is golden brown.

3. Stir in butter and vanilla. Microwave on HIGH 1½ minutes.

4. Stir in baking soda (mixture will foam up) and immediately pour on prepared baking sheet; do not scrape side of bowl. Stretch as thin as possible, using 2 forks.

5. Cool, then break in pieces. Store tightly covered.

Makes about ¾ pound

Hint: If kitchen is cold, warm baking sheet before pouring out brittle. It will spread more easily and will be thinner.

Easy Microwave Fudge

Full of nuts and with a mild chocolate flavor, this fudge is a crowd pleaser.

> 3¾ cups powdered sugar
> ½ cup unsweetened cocoa powder
> ¼ cup evaporated milk
> 2 teaspoons vanilla
> ½ cup butter or margarine, cut into pieces
> ¾ cup chopped pecans

1. Line 8-inch square pan with buttered foil; set aside.

2. Sift powdered sugar and cocoa into 2-quart microwave-safe bowl. Stir in milk and vanilla. Top with butter. Microwave on HIGH 3 minutes or until butter melts and mixture is hot.

3. Stir in pecans. Spread into prepared pan. Refrigerate until firm.

4. Remove fudge from pan by lifting out foil. Cut into squares.

5. Store in refrigerator.

Makes about 1½ pounds

Microwave Chocolate Mints

The layers of mint and chocolate make these pretty.

1 package (10 ounces) mint chocolate chips
¼ cup butter or margarine, cut into pieces
10 ounces white confectioner's coating
¼ cup butter or margarine, cut into pieces
½ teaspoon peppermint extract
Green food coloring

1. Line 8-inch square pan with buttered foil; set aside.

2. Microwave chips in small microwave-safe bowl on HIGH 1 minute. Stir; add ¼ cup butter.

3. Microwave on HIGH 1½ minutes; stir until smooth. If chips are not completely melted, microwave on HIGH 30 seconds more. Spread in prepared pan. Refrigerate until firm.

4. Combine confectioner's coating and remaining ¼ cup butter in clean small microwave-safe bowl. Microwave on HIGH 2 minutes, stirring after every minute. If not completely melted, microwave on HIGH 30 seconds more.

5. Stir in peppermint extract. Add food coloring, a few drops at a time, until desired color is obtained. Cool slightly. Pour evenly over chocolate layer. Score mints into 2×1-inch bars with knife. Refrigerate until almost firm.

6. Remove mints from pan by lifting out foil. Cut into bars. Refrigerate until firm.   *Makes 32 bars*

Hint: Bars are easier to cut without breaking if chocolate is not completely firm.

Nut Clusters

Macadamia nuts add a lot of flavor to the chocolate, but any nut can be used.

1 cup milk chocolate chips
2 squares (1 ounce each) unsweetened chocolate,
**   chopped**
1 cup macadamia nuts

1. Line baking sheet with buttered waxed paper; set aside.

2. Microwave chips and chopped chocolate in small microwave-safe bowl on HIGH 2 minutes, stirring after every minute. If not completely melted, microwave on HIGH 30 seconds more.

3. Stir in nuts. Drop by teaspoonfuls on prepared baking sheet. Let stand until firm.   *Makes about ¾ pound*

Microwave Chocolate Mints;
Nut Clusters

FRUIT
❋
FANTASIES

Wire rack, top to bottom: Candied Orange Peel (page 87); Fruit Bars (page 86) and Stuffed Dates (page 86); Table top: Strawberry-Applesauce Jellies (page 87); Bowl: Apricot Balls (page 84)

Coconut Balls

Rolled in coconut, this chewy candy has a fresh orange flavor.

½ cup golden raisins, chopped
½ cup pitted prunes or dates, chopped
½ cup graham cracker crumbs
½ cup powdered sugar
1 tablespoon grated orange peel
½ cup sweetened condensed milk
1 cup shredded coconut

1. Combine raisins, prunes, crumbs, sugar and peel in medium bowl. Stir in condensed milk. Refrigerate until firm enough to shape into balls, about 30 minutes.

2. Place coconut in shallow bowl.

3. For each candy, shape scant 1 tablespoonful of the mixture into 1-inch ball. Roll in coconut.

4. Store in refrigerator.

Makes about 30 balls

Papaya-Orange Jellies

Fun and delicious to eat, these are also very easy to make.

4 envelopes (¼ ounce each) unflavored gelatin
½ cup sugar
1½ cups (12 ounces) papaya nectar
1 can (6 ounces) frozen orange juice concentrate, thawed

1. Lightly oil 8-inch square pan; set aside.

2. Combine unflavored gelatin and sugar in medium saucepan. Stir in nectar and orange juice concentrate. Let stand 5 minutes to soften gelatin.

3. Bring to a boil over medium heat, stirring constantly; boil until gelatin is completely dissolved. Pour into prepared pan. Refrigerate until firm.

4. Dip pan in warm water 15 seconds. Cut into 2×1-inch bars or use cookie cutters to cut designs. Remove from pan. (Scraps can be chopped and mixed with whipped cream for desserts.) Refrigerate until ready to serve.

Makes 32 bars

Coconut Balls

Apricot Balls

Add a rich orange color and the delicious tartness of apricots to a holiday party with these easy confections.

8 ounces dried apricots
1 cup flaked coconut
¼ cup sweetened condensed milk
Additional flaked coconut for rolling (optional)

1. Chop apricots in food processor. Add coconut; process until combined. Add condensed milk; process until combined. Pour into pie pan. Refrigerate until firm enough to shape into balls, about 30 minutes.

2. Line baking sheet with buttered waxed paper; set aside.

3. Place additional coconut in shallow bowl.

4. For each candy, shape scant 1 tablespoonful of the mixture into 1-inch ball. Roll in coconut. Place balls on prepared baking sheet. Refrigerate until firm.

5. Store in refrigerator. *Makes about 22 balls*

Hint: Leftover sweetened condensed milk will keep several days, tightly covered, in the refrigerator. Use in coffee, fruit salads or dessert sauces.

Chocolate-Covered Raisins

Golden or dark raisins can be used in this no-fuss recipe.

2 cups (11½ ounces) milk chocolate chips
1 square (1 ounce) unsweetened chocolate,
chopped
1 tablespoon shortening
2 cups raisins

1. Line baking sheet with buttered waxed paper; set aside.

2. Melt chips and chopped chocolate with shortening in medium saucepan over low heat, stirring constantly. Stir in raisins.

3. Drop individual raisins or drop in clusters from spoon onto prepared baking sheet. Let stand until firm. *Makes about 1½ pounds*

Top: Apricot Balls
Bottom: Chocolate-Covered Raisins

Stuffed Dates

The rich filling in these sweet dates makes them an elegant after-dinner treat.

1 can (7 ounces) almond paste
1 tablespoon amaretto liqueur (optional)
Food coloring (optional)
About 30 pitted dates

1. Combine almond paste and liqueur in small bowl. Add food coloring, a few drops at a time, until desired color is obtained.

2. Spoon mixture into pastry bag fitted with large star tip. Pipe into centers of dates.

3. Store in refrigerator. *Makes about 30 dates*

Hint: Piping the almond paste mixture is the easiest way to fill the dates.

Fruit Bars

Chock-full of fruit, this "candy" bar makes a great change of pace from traditional chocolate bars.

1 cup chopped figs
1 cup chopped dates
1 cup chopped dried pears
1 cup finely chopped pecans
¼ cup orange marmalade

1. Butter 8-inch square pan; set aside.

2. Combine all ingredients in medium bowl. Press mixture in prepared pan. Refrigerate until set.

3. Cut into bars. Store in refrigerator. *Makes 32 bars*

Hint: To prepare without a food processor, finely chop fruit and nuts. Combine fruit and nuts in medium bowl. Stir in marmalade. Proceed as directed in step 3.

Candied Orange Peel

For a special treat, dip one end of these candied peels into melted milk chocolate.

**3 large oranges
Water
3 cups sugar, divided**

1. Remove peel from oranges in strips; remove white membrane. Cut peel into ¼- to ½-inch-wide strips.

2. Place strips in heavy, medium saucepan; cover with cold water. Bring to a boil over medium heat; drain and repeat 2 more times. Set aside orange peel.

3. Line baking sheet with buttered waxed paper; set aside.

4. Combine ½ cup water and 1½ cups of the sugar in same saucepan. Cook over medium heat, stirring constantly, until sugar dissolves.

5. Add orange peel. Cook 10 to 15 minutes until slightly translucent, stirring occasionally.

6. Place remaining 1½ cups sugar in shallow bowl. Place orange peel in bowl, a few strips at a time; toss to coat. Dry peel overnight on wire rack. Break into small pieces.
Makes about ½ pound

Strawberry-Applesauce Jellies

Not too sweet, these have a beautiful red color and a slightly chewy texture.

**1 package (3 ounces) strawberry-flavored gelatin
3 envelopes (¼ ounce each) unflavored gelatin
⅓ cup sugar
2 cups sweetened applesauce**

1. Lightly oil 8-inch square pan; set aside.

2. Combine strawberry gelatin, unflavored gelatin and sugar in medium saucepan. Stir in applesauce. Let stand 5 minutes to soften gelatin.

3. Bring to a boil over medium heat, stirring constantly; boil until gelatin is completely dissolved. Pour into prepared pan. Refrigerate until firm.

4. Dip pan in warm water 15 seconds. Cut into 1-inch squares or use cookie cutters to cut into designs. Remove from pan. (Scraps can be chopped and mixed with whipped cream for desserts.) Refrigerate until ready to serve.
Makes 64 squares

GRAB-BAG
❁
GOODIES

Box: Sugar-Free Coconut Balls (page 92); Plate: Orange Creams (page 94); Bittersweet Chocolate Mints (page 92); Canister: Sugared Nuts (page 90)

Sugared Nuts

Any combination of nuts can be used for these sugary treats.

1 cup sugar
½ cup water
2½ cups unsalted mixed nuts
1 teaspoon vanilla

1. Grease baking sheet; set aside.

2. Combine sugar and water in medium saucepan. Cook, stirring constantly, over medium heat until sugar dissolves.

3. Add nuts and vanilla. Cook, stirring occasionally, until water evaporates and nuts are sugary, about 12 minutes.

4. Spread nuts on prepared baking sheet, separating nuts. Let stand until cooled.   *Makes about 1 pound*

Almond-Coconut Balls

These rich-tasting candies make an elegant presentation.

1 can (7 ounces) almond paste
⅓ cup powdered sugar
1 cup flaked coconut
1 to 2 teaspoons water
7 ounces pastel-colored confectioner's coating

1. Line baking sheet with buttered waxed paper; set aside.

2. Combine almond paste, sugar and coconut in a medium bowl. Stir in water if mixture is dry.

3. For each candy, shape scant 1 tablespoonful of the mixture into 1-inch ball. Place balls on prepared baking sheet. Refrigerate until set, about 30 minutes.

4. Melt confectioner's coating in bowl over hot, not boiling water, stirring constantly.

5. Dip balls, using dipping fork or skewer, in coating to cover. Remove excess coating by scraping bottom of ball across rim on saucepan. Return to baking sheet. Reheat coating if it gets too thick. Refrigerate until set, about 30 minutes.   *Makes about 24 balls*

Top: Sugared Nuts
Bottom: Almond-Coconut Balls

Sugar-Free Coconut Balls

These creamy candies contain no sugar, yet are full of flavor and easy to make.

1 package (8 ounces) light cream cheese,
    softened
2 teaspoons liquid sugar substitute
½ teaspoon coconut extract
1 cup unsweetened flaked or shredded coconut
    Grated unsweetened chocolate, unsweetened
    cocoa powder, toasted sesame seeds or
    toasted chopped almonds for rolling

1. Beat cream cheese, sugar substitute and coconut extract in medium bowl with electric mixer until smooth. Stir in coconut. Refrigerate until slightly firm, about 20 minutes.

2. Place grated chocolate in shallow bowl.

3. For each candy, shape scant 1 tablespoonful of the mixture into 1-inch ball. Roll balls in chocolate.

4. Store in refrigerator.   *Makes about 28 balls*

Sugar-Free Almond Balls: Substitute chopped toasted almonds for the coconut and ¼ teaspoon almond extract for the coconut extract. Roll in grated chocolate.

Bittersweet Chocolate Mints

These soft mints have a rich chocolate flavor.

3 squares (1 ounce each) unsweetened chocolate,
    coarsely chopped
½ cup semisweet chocolate chips
3 packets sugar substitute
1 teaspoon peppermint extract

1. Line 9×5-inch loaf pan with buttered foil; set aside.

2. Melt chocolate and chips in medium bowl over hot, not boiling water, stirring constantly.

3. Stir in sugar substitute and peppermint extract; mix well. Pour into prepared pan. Score mints with knife into 1-inch squares. Refrigerate until firm.

4. Cut into squares. Store in refrigerator until just before serving.
Makes about ¼ pound

Top: Sugar-Free Coconut Balls
Bottom: Bittersweet Chocolate Mints

Orange Creams

For a sweet orange taste, try these delicious creamy, soft candies.

> 2¼ to 2½ cups powdered sugar
> 1 tablespoon grated orange peel
> 3 tablespoons frozen orange juice concentrate*
> Additional powdered sugar for rolling

1. Line baking sheet with buttered waxed paper; set aside.

2. Combine 2¼ cups sugar, orange peel and orange juice concentrate in small bowl, adding more sugar if needed to make a stiff dough.

3. Form dough into ball; wrap in plastic wrap. Refrigerate 30 minutes.

4. Roll out dough into ¼-inch thickness on surface covered with powdered sugar.

5. Cut into 1½-inch shapes. Arrange on prepared baking sheet. Refrigerate, uncovered, overnight.

6. Store in refrigerator in tightly sealed container between layers of waxed paper.   *Makes about 36 creams*

Hint: Keep refrigerated to make serving easier.

*Or, substitute any flavor frozen juice concentrate.

Spiced Nuts

After baking, the pecans are crisp and crunchy with a hint of spice.

> 1 egg white
> 2 tablespoons sugar
> 1 teaspoon ground cinnamon
> ½ teaspoon ground allspice
> 1¾ cups pecan halves

1. Preheat oven to 325°F. Grease baking sheet; set aside.

2. Beat egg white in small bowl with electric mixer until soft peaks form. Beat in sugar, cinnamon and allspice. Stir in pecans until coated.

3. Spread pecans on prepared baking sheet, separating pecans. Bake about 12 minutes or until crisp. Let stand until cooled.   *Makes about ¼ pound*

INDEX